THE LITTLE BLACK BOOK

Modern Dating Etiquette for Men
or
How to Get the Girl and Not Lose Her

by
Ditzy

Warning! This book should not be read by anyone with a weak heart, a weak bladder or for those suffering from chronic seriousness.

TIPS FROM THE ICEBERG.

Hello boys. This is an essential Little Black Book for those who are floundering around either without a girlfriend or without success in their sexual lives, or for any man who is coming up against rejection from the opposite sex.

We women have read a zillion books on how to attract the right man. But you guys? Perhaps you are too shy to ask, too intimidated - or maybe you think you are just perfect the way you are.

Trust me, when it comes to regular manners and bedroom manners – the tools for success with women – there is always room for improvement.

Whatever - we women know you need help and suspect that you are secretly longing for a few tips...

Remember we only want to help....

BASIC GOOD MANNERS.

We all know the golden rule - treat others as you would like to be treated yourself.

However, when it comes to getting the woman of your dreams you have to go that bit further....remember, manners are free. You do not have to be wealthy to have decent manners. It does not matter how fat, skinny, shy, or what color your skin is. All human beings are capable of treating each other with respect.

Maybe you just can't get that date...

Maybe your marriage is going through a rocky patch and you feel like your wife hates you...

Maybe women take a step backwards when you approach them...

Let's see what you can do about it to turn your luck around.

EXERCISE.

Like manners, exercise is free. Anybody can exercise. There is no excuse for being out of shape.

If you think you can get away with a blobby tummy and love handles, you're wrong. Okay, maybe if you are Jack Nicholson or a trillionaire, you'll have women trembling, but otherwise you'd better get your act together.

As well as looking better, you will feel better.

The reason that most people suffer from back pain is because they don't do enough exercise. I know it's a pain in neck (pun intended) but it just has to be done. Don't be lazy! You can do a big part of your daily quota in little ways, like choosing to walk up the stairs instead of going by escalator, or walking instead of driving.

Remember, one important fact: we women are *allowed* to have a few curves, pouches and extra layers. We are made that way. Plus, we give birth and you don't. Our bodies are designed to store fat and yours aren't. So don't you dare go criticising our little tummies! And don't go using lack of time as an excuse.

Ways to stay in shape:

- Running. It's free and you get to see the scenery too.

- Press ups and push ups. You don't even have to leave the house or get changed. You'll be amazed with only 10 minutes a day.

- Yoga. If you're a single man, there is no better way to meet a girl. Why sweat it out in the gym with sweaty men, lying about their conquests, when you could be the only man in a room full of skimpily dressed females?

- Lifting things for women. A lot of men shirk their duty by disappearing into busyness or illness at the crucial hour. You cannot imagine the gold stars you earn when you help us move apartments or lift a heavy piece of furniture. It is literally a weight off our minds, both mentally and physically. Get those biceps into shape!

- Whatever exercise you choose, concentrate on the belly. A flabby one is the biggest turn-off for a woman. Beware – don't get obsessed - most females are not attracted to bull necks, twenty-four packs and pecs bigger than our own breasts.

YOUR MOUTH.

What comes out of the mouth verbally is not the only thing that boys have to keep in check. Oral hygiene and attractive teeth are both a must. OK, so you had a series of bad dentists when you were young; you threw your retainer across the floor and never wore it - your teeth are crooked and full of fillings. But that is no reason to have cream-coloured teeth or let them be etched in brown or to go around with stinky breath!

Of all the sinful smells, (farting, B.O, smelly feet) bad breath is the worst. And there is no excuse. I have seen millionaires with yellow teeth. Why? Why would you do that yourself? Why d'you think we think George Clooney and Ashton Kutcher are gorgeous? Can you imagine them with sorry looking teeth? Even alternative, anti-fashion do-their-own-thing stars like David Bowie have dealt with their teeth.

- Brush your teeth every morning and night, preferably with an electric (no worn out heads) toothbrush.

- Flossing. It prevents gum disease and helps reduce staining, not to mention bad breath.

- Bleach or laser your teeth if they are anything less than white.

- Go to the dentist every six months or at least once a year.

- Get your teeth cleaned by a really good hygienist.

- Chewing sugarless gum after sweet things helps reduce cavities and monitors bad breath.

- Carry a fold-up toothbrush around with you or have a spare one at work. You'll need it at opportune or inopportune moments, believe me.

- Last but not least. Brush your tongue as well as your teeth as that's where stinkyness lurks.

Investing money in your teeth is money well spent. You get one set, (baby teeth don't count) so look after them. An attractive man with wonderful teeth = sexy. A handsome man with dirty teeth = disappointment. Even if your teeth are an orthodontists nightmare, at least let them be clean and not beige.

HAIR (or lack of).

A lot of men have unwanted hair in many places and lack of wanted hair in others. If you are going bald, consider shaving it all off. Think of how sexy Yul Brynner was in his prime. Even Telly Savalas had women throwing their panties at him, way back when. Andre Agassi, Bruce Willis, Billy Zane – have all gone bald and look great! There is nothing worse than threading thin hairs across a sparse head - or balding men with long hair. (Sorry, the pirate look is out of the question for you guys.)

Likewise, if you have an extremely hairy, beast-like body it is nowadays easy to deal with.

No no's are:

a.) So much hair on backs and shoulders you can't see the skin beneath.
b.) Hairs coming out of nostrils and ears.
Get it plucked, lazered or waxed. Or, do it yourself at home.

Worried about pain? Don't be a baby. An electric zap here or there, or the rip of strip-wax ain't nothing compared to childbirth, honey, so get over it and book yourself an appointment at the salon.

UNDERWEAR.

Socks.

- Buy natural-fibre socks so that foot odor is reduced. Avoid nylon or man-made fibres. Have extra bundles of socks in your closet so you don't run out (assuming that like most men you are lazy about doing laundry).

- Change socks EVERY day and if you go out for the evening, change them again.

- Clip your toenails in PRIVATE and throw away debris.

- Keep your sneakers clean. Put them in the washing machine every so often – use 'odor eaters' and throw the shoes away when they get manky.

Boxer briefs versus old-fashioned Y-fronts.

We girls prefer boxer briefs but not when they are too enormous or too squeezed tight. Broken elastic, holes or stains? THROW THEM AWAY. If they are Y-fronts, they'd better be good quality, 100 per cent cotton and plain coloured. NO PATTERNS! No pimp penis holders (e.g. cut away mini briefs) especially black, unless you are an Italian beachcomber with a comb, luring tourists out of the sea and into your medallion bed.

BATHROOM MANNERS.

In a perfect world, boys would be relegated to their own bathrooms and leave ours un-tainted. However, if there is only one bathroom:

- Aim well. If you miss-fire, wipe up the mess so nobody knows. Even if you live alone, do you want visitors knowing about your golden pee stains everywhere?

- If you empty your bowels and the toilet bowl is smeared with breakfast, take two seconds to clean it up. Do you want people seeing the evidence? You never know when a guest might drop by.

- Put the toilet seat **down** after use. It looks nicer and it shows consideration, not to mention good Feng Shui. (Do you want your money, love life etc disappearing down the toilet?) However strongly you feel about the seat being up - remember it is the number one bathroom etiquette complaint on women's lists. If you leave it up, we girls take it as a personal affront and think you're doing it on purpose to upset us. Are you?

- Clean up the ring around the bath or the dirty footprints (hello? did you even *wash* your feet?) after a shower. Do you really want us knowing just how filthy you were before your scrub?

- Fold up towels after use. Leaving them scrumpled around in piles on the floor, screams slobby-ness and laziness. Folding them takes two to ten seconds.

- If you shave, rinse around the sink so little hairs aren't everywhere. Would you like to see our underarm hairs etc around? The same goes for all hairs - whoosh those short and curlies down the drain.

- Made a big stink? HELLO? Open the window! If there isn't one, light some incense.

- The fact that I'm writing this proves that it needs to be said: remember to always flush.

BAD HABITS.

If you saw a lovely looking girl picking her nose and farting, maybe you'd decide she wasn't so attractive after all. What makes you think you're different? Do your dirty deeds in private.

- Nose picking or any other orifice exploring; do not wipe your filth on surfaces, curtains etc. Get a tissue and throw it away.

- Burping. No we don't think it's manly. With burps anti-social smells are released.

- Farting. Only dogs can get away with farting on purpose, in public. Are you a dog?

- Feet picking - do it in private.

- Spot squeezing - yes we know it's satisfying when the puss hits the mirror on those one-off, perfect-explosion kinda days, but keep your excitement and the evidence to yourself.

Even if you've got the girl and she's living with you, don't think you can get away with filthy habits for long. She'll notice and she'll start fantasizing about other men or even about living alone with a real dog. Is that what you want?

TABLE MANNERS.

It is amazing how people believe they can eat and talk at the same time and seem interesting and attractive to others. Not only do people not want to hear what they say, but they actually want to close their eyes. Basically, don't be grotesque.

- If you want to partake in scintillating conversation, take smaller mouthfuls. That way you'll make more time for yourself to talk in-between bites.

- Close your mouth when you chew, even if you are not talking.

- Don't scrape your plate, making horrible noises (like nails on a blackboard) and marking your hosts (all for that matter your own) plates.

- No scrumming. No helping yourself before you have offered food and drink to others first. Even if you are greedy and selfish, others don't have to perceive you that way. Top up other people's wine and water first.

- Pass the bread, the salt etc along. Don't wait for others to ask you.

- However delicious dinner is, don't make wolfy slurping sounds, unless you are alone with your dog.

- When your mouth is NOT full, compliment your hostess's/wife's/girlfriend's cooking.

- Do not cut spaghetti or omelettes with a knife – it's just not done. Unless of course, you're an Angry Young Man from the 1960s dining with the ghost of John Osborne or haunted by the spirit of Ted Hughes.

DATING.

Unless you have your eye on Ms. Career 2084, if you don't want to seem like Scrooge on your first date:

- Always offer to pay for the meal unless:
  a.) she invited you out especially or
  b.) she absolutely insists upon paying, or going Dutch.
  (If you're broke take her on a picnic or cook her spaghetti at home.)

- Don't douse yourself with an entire bottle of 'odor' cologne

- It seems like a really obvious thing to say but you'd be surprised: don't bring a third party along.

- Don't eat a garlic sandwich either the same day or the day before. That includes chorizo sausages.

- Have a plan, even if you want things to seem casual. It's very irritating for women when her date says, "Where shall we go?" At least give a list of options.

- Don't be more than 5 minutes late to pick her up (15 mins Latin countries) or at least call ahead if delayed. For Goodness sake don't arrive too early either (and by the way - yes, you should offer to pick her up at her home.)

- Don't lie. Don't borrow a friend's Mercedes, pretending it's yours, and don't fib about what you do or don't do for a living. Liars are tedious.

- Don't launch into post-mortems on past relationships. We don't want to know about all your exes (well we do, and we will find out - but all in good time). If you bang on about your exes, we'll think you're still banging them, in love with them or that you're bitter and twisted or worse, all of the above.

- Listen to yourself. Are you saying the word 'I' too often? Remember you're taking HER on a date, not yourself.

- Open the door for her, pull-out her chair at the table and help her on and off with her coat. Keep her glass filled with whatever she's drinking.

- Compliment her.

- Don't name-drop or talk about how much money you earn, or how you live overseas for tax reasons.

- Don't be rude about other people (not yet, anyway).

- Walk her home, drive her home or call a cab (if you pay the driver in advance you'll score extra brownie points). If you drive her home, wait until you see her unlock her front door and that she is safely inside – or MUCH better still, get out of the car and walk her to the front door. Don't push your way into her lobby or hall – let yourself be invited, or not, as the case may be.

- If you do sleep with her, call her the next day to say thank-you for the nice time, even if you never want see her again. If you call her, she won't think you're an asshole and she won't be rude about you to her friends.

- Also, remember, if you don't call her, she might even try to boil your bunny.

IN BED.

Are you a gentleman or a chauvinist? Even if you are a chauvinist and she is attracted to you for your he-man qualities, there is one place where you have to play the gentlemen's role: in the bedroom or wherever else you choose to have sex. If you want be considered a good lover there is one golden rule:

LADIES FIRST

If you consider your own pleasures before hers, you will be thought of, quite simply, as **bad in bed**. Do you want to walk around with that tag? Believe me, and I'm sure you do, women talk. Even if you are ugly or even if you have a bad body, you can still be good in bed. Yes, it is something that all men can aspire to and something that all women want. Good in bed means:

- Fore-play. Caressing her body and making her feel special. Listening to what she likes and acting on it.

- Patience. You are not in a race. It may take time to get her really turned on. No yawning or sighing or showing signs of boredom.

- Talk. Tell her she is gorgeous and sexy. Total silence is a turn-off.

- Remember she has a whole body and not just breasts and orifices. Pay attention to her entire body, from head to toe.

- Unless you're the type that can keep going - let her come first. Take your time and control yourself. Remember the equation:

<u>man coming first</u> = <u>selfish in bed</u>

= **BAD IN BED**

It's your choice

P.S: Most women have faked orgasm at least once in their lives. Some do it on a regular basis. Think it hasn't happened to you? As Sally said to Harry: "You do the math." Don't be a statistic.

P.P.S: Premature ejaculators – tip: have a quick, private jerk-off before you begin.

ONCE YOU ARE DATING HER...

If you want to keep her sweet, bear in mind all of the above and:

- Don't flirt outrageously with other women in front of her.

- Don't make promises you can't keep.

- Don't lie ~ female intuition will catch you in the end.

- Don't ask her to map read and then explode at the results.

- Don't ask her how many men she's slept with. She'll either lie or tell the truth. Trust me, ignorance is bliss.

- Don't play a video game and then tell her how busy you are.

- Don't tell her "I'll do it tomorrow."

- Don't tell her she looks tired.

- Do buy her flowers.

- Do wear earphones when you're watching your favorite game on TV.

- Do make her dinner or surprise her with a picnic.

- Do run her a bath when she's had a long hard day at work.

- Do bring her a cup of coffee or tea in the morning in bed.

- Do change the light bulbs without being asked (big brownie points).

- Do have sex or cuddles with her in the morning.

- Do love her dog, her cat or her kid(s).

BE NICE.

"Treat 'em mean, keep 'em keen" may seem to work for you for a few years but WAKEY WAKEY while you're busy being an asshole (e.g. indecisive, "needing space," being unfaithful etc.) all the sweet, lovely girls are getting snapped up. You'll be left with the crazies, the neurotics, the eleventh and thirteenth-go-rounders and the psychotic ex-models. Then even *they* will get bored of you and run off to find a NICE person. You'll realise in the end:

IT PAYS TO BE A DECENT GUY.

GOOD LUCK BOYS - remember, we women only want to help!

Our happiness is your happiness.

Remember that.

Printed in Great Britain
by Amazon